Our Lady Says:

Pray The Creed

By Rev. Albert J.M. Shamon

Our Lady Says:

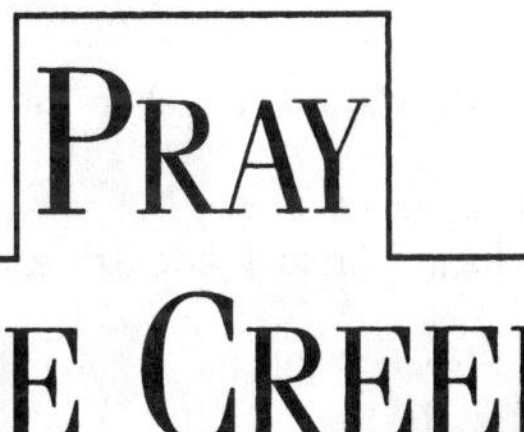

PRAY THE CREED

By Rev. Albert J.M. Shamon

"Be thou faithful unto death and I will give thee the Crown of Life."

(Rev. 2:10)

Published by
CMJ MARIAN PUBLISHERS
AND DISTRIBUTORS
P.O. Box 661
Oak Lawn, IL 60454

Published by CMJ Marian Publishers and Distributors

For additional copies contact:
Your local Christian bookstore, or write:

CMJ Marian Publishers
P.O. Box 661
Oak Lawn, IL 60454

Copyright © 1990 Fr. Albert Shamon

Library of Congress Catalog Card No.: 00-102755

ISBN: 1-891280-11-2

Publisher:
CMJ Marian Publishers
and Distributors
Post Office Box 661
Oak Lawn, Illinois 60454
Tel: 708-636-2995 / Fax: 708-636-2855
Toll Free: 1-888-636-6799
http://www.cmjbooks.com
jwby@aol.com

CONTENTS

PREFACE

On June 27, 1981, during the sixth apparition of Our Lady at Medjugorje, the children recited the seven Our Father's, Hail Mary's, and Glory Be's according to the Croatian custom in honor of the seven sorrows of Mary. It was on this occasion that Our Lady said: "Continue to recite these prayers, but also add the Creed."

Later on, she asked that they say the Creed as part of their morning prayers (1/27/84).

On February 10, 1982, in her diary, Vicka, the oldest of the seers, said that the prayer Our Lady preferred is the Creed. "When we recite it, the Blessed Virgin does not cease to smile. I think that no one has seen her happier than during this prayer."

Again, Mary said: "The most beautiful prayer is the Creed."

Why? Because the most important thing is to believe. Paradise was lost through a lack of faith: our first parents believed Satan and not God. So an act of faith is needed to regain the paradise lost.

And the summary of our Faith is the Creed.

I do hope and pray that this little booklet will deepen your knowledge of and love for and devotion to our glorious Faith.

Feast of St. Martha
July 29, 1989
Albert Joseph Mary Shamon

The Holy Face of Jesus

The Veil of Veronica
Preserved in St. Peter's Basilica in Rome

"By offering My Face to My Eternal Father, nothing will be refused, and the conversion of many sinners will be obtained."
- Our Lord to Sr. Marie de Saint-Pierre
(November 1846)

DEVOTION TO THE HOLY FACE OF JESUS

On November 24, 1843, Our Lord spoke the following words to the French Carmelite, **Sr. Marie de Saint-Pierre**: "The earth is covered with crimes. The violation of the first three Commandments of God has irritated My Father. The Holy Name of God blasphemed, and the Holy Day of the Lord profaned, fills up the measure in iniquities. These sins have risen unto the Throne of God and provoked His wrath which will soon burst forth if His justice be not appeased. At no time have these crimes reached such a pitch." Our Lord appeared several times to Sister Marie to ask for reparation to be done to His Holy Face. These revelations have the full approval of the Catholic Church.

Sister Marie was given a vision in which she saw the Sacred Heart of Jesus delightfully wounded by the "Golden Arrow" as torrents of graces streamed from It for the conversion of sinners.

The Golden Arrow Prayer

Dictated by Our Lord to Sr. Marie of St.Peter

May the Most Holy, Most Sacred, Most Adorable, Most Incomprehensible and Ineffable Name of God be always praised, blessed, loved, adored and glorified, in Heaven, on earth, and under the earth, by all the creatures of God and by the Sacred Heart of Our Lord Jesus Christ in the Most Holy Sacrament of the altar. Amen.

Our Lord told Sr. Marie of St. Peter on March 16, 1844, "Oh if you only knew what great merit you acquire by saying even once, **'Admirable is the Name of God,'** in the spirit of reparation for blasphemy." (say often)

Eternal Father, we offer Thee the adorable Face of Thy well-beloved Son, for the honor and glory of Thy Holy Name and for the salvation of souls.

O Jesus, through the merits of Thy Holy Face, have pity on us, and on the whole world. (three times)

Promises of Our Lord to Sr. Marie of St. Peter

1. By My Holy Face you shall work wonders.

2. All those who honor My Holy Face in a spirit of reparation will by so doing perform the office of the pious Veronica.

3. According to the care you take in making Reparation to My Face, disfigured by blasphemies, so will I take care of yours, which has been disfigured by sin. I will reprint My image and render it as beautiful as it was on leaving the baptismal font.

4. Our Lord has promised me for all those who defend His cause in this Work of Reparation, by words, by prayers, or in writing, that He will defend them before His Father; at their death He will purify their souls by effacing all the blots of sin and will restore to them their primitive beauty.

5. Our Lord has promised me that He will imprint His Divine likeness on the souls of those who honor His Holy Face.

The Holy Face Medal

Sister Maria Pierina de Micheli (died in 1945 – beatified May 30, 2010) was urged in many visions by the Blessed Mother and Jesus Himself to spread the devotion to the Holy Face. The Blessed Virgin Mary appeared to her holding a Scapular which on one piece bore the image from the Holy Shroud with the words "Ilumina Domine Vultum Tuum Super Nos" (May the light of Thy Face, O Lord, shine upon us) and on the other a Host surrounded by rays and the words "Mane Nobiscum Domine" (Stay with us, O Lord). Our Lady promised: "all who shall wear a Scapular like this and make, if possible, a visit to the Blessed Sacrament every Tuesday in reparation for the outrages that the Holy Face of my Son Jesus received during His Passion and is still receiving in the Holy Eucharist every day, will be strengthened in the Faith and be made ready to defend it, will overcome all difficulties, internal and external and will have a peaceful death under the loving gaze of my Divine Son."

Sr. Pierina felt inspired and obtained permission to have a medal cast which Our Lady approved of and granted the same favors and promises as those of the Scapular.

The first medal of the Holy Face was offered to Pope Pius XII who approved the devotion and the medal. On April 17, 1958, he declared the Tuesday before Ash Wednesday (Shrove Tuesday) as the Feast of the Holy Face of Jesus as Our Lord had requested.

The Holy Face Medal

Sister Maria Pierina de Micheli (died in 1945 – beatified May 30, 2010) was urged in many visions by the Blessed Mother and Jesus Himself to spread the devotion to the Holy Face. The Blessed Virgin Mary appeared to her holding a Scapular which on one piece bore the image from the Holy Shroud with the words "Ilumina Domine Vultum Tuum Super Nos" (May the light of Thy Face, O Lord, shine upon us) and on the other a Host surrounded by rays and the words "Mane Nobiscum Domine" (Stay with us, O Lord). Our Lady promised: "all who shall wear a Scapular like this and make, if possible, a visit to the Blessed Sacrament every Tuesday in reparation for the outrages that the Holy Face of my Son Jesus received during His Passion and is still receiving in the Holy Eucharist every day, will be strengthened in the Faith and be made ready to defend it, will overcome all difficulties, internal and external and will have a peaceful death under the loving gaze of my Divine Son."

Sr. Pierina felt inspired and obtained permission to have a medal cast which Our Lady approved of and granted the same favors and promises as those of the Scapular.

The first medal of the Holy Face was offered to Pope Pius XII who approved the devotion and the medal. On April 17, 1958, he declared the Tuesday before Ash Wednesday (Shrove Tuesday) as the Feast of the Holy Face of Jesus as Our Lord had requested.

The Holy Face of Jesus

The Veil of Veronica

Preserved in St. Peter's Basilica in Rome

"By offering My Face to My Eternal Father, nothing will be refused, and the conversion of many sinners will be obtained."

- Our Lord to Sr. Marie de Saint-Pierre
(November 1846)

DEVOTION TO THE HOLY FACE OF JESUS

On November 24, 1843, Our Lord spoke the following words to the French Carmelite, **Sr. Marie de Saint-Pierre**: "The earth is covered with crimes. The violation of the first three Commandments of God has irritated My Father. The Holy Name of God blasphemed, and the Holy Day of the Lord profaned, fills up the measure in iniquities. These sins have risen unto the Throne of God and provoked His wrath which will soon burst forth if His justice be not appeased. At no time have these crimes reached such a pitch." Our Lord appeared several times to Sister Marie to ask for reparation to be done to His Holy Face. These revelations have the full approval of the Catholic Church.

Sister Marie was given a vision in which she saw the Sacred Heart of Jesus delightfully wounded by the "Golden Arrow" as torrents of graces streamed from It for the conversion of sinners.

The Golden Arrow Prayer

Dictated by Our Lord to Sr. Marie of St.Peter

May the Most Holy, Most Sacred, Most Adorable, Most Incomprehensible and Ineffable Name of God be always praised, blessed, loved, adored and glorified, in Heaven, on earth, and under the earth, by all the creatures of God and by the Sacred Heart of Our Lord Jesus Christ in the Most Holy Sacrament of the altar. Amen.

Our Lord told Sr. Marie of St. Peter on March 16, "Oh if you only knew what great merit you acquire by saying even once, **'Admirable is the Name of God,'** in the spirit of reparation for blasphemy." (say often)

Eternal Father, we offer Thee the adorable Face of Thy well-beloved Son, for the honor and glory of Thy Holy Name and for the salvation of souls.

O Jesus, through the merits of Thy Holy Face, have pity on us, and on the whole world. (three times)

Promises of Our Lord to Sr. Marie of St. Peter

1. By My Holy Face you shall work wonders.

2. All those who honor My Holy Face in a spirit of reparation will by so doing perform the office of the pious Veronica.

3. According to the care you take in making Reparation to My Face, disfigured by blasphemies, so will I take care of yours, which has been disfigured by sin. I will reprint My image and render it as beautiful as it was on leaving the baptismal font.

4. Our Lord has promised me for all those who defend His cause in this Work of Reparation, by words, by prayers, or in writing, that He will defend them before His Father; at their death He will purify their souls by effacing all the blots of sin and will restore to them their primitive bea

5. Our Lord has promised me that He will imprint Hi likeness on the souls of those who honor His Ho

Good Night To Our Blessed Mother

Night is falling dear Mother, the long day is o'er!
And before thy loved image I am kneeling once more
To thank thee for keeping me safe through the day
To ask thee this night to keep evil away.
Many times have I fallen today, Mother Dear,
Many graces neglected, since last I knelt here;
Wilt thou not in pity, my own Mother mild,
Ask Jesus to pardon the sins of thy child?
I am going to rest, for the day's work is done,
Its hours and its moments have passed one by one;
And the God who will judge me has noted them all,
He has numbered each grace, He has counted each fall.
In His book they are written against the last day,
O Mother, ask Jesus to wash them away;
For one drop of His blood which for sinners was spilt,
Is sufficient to cleanse the whole world of its guilt.
And if ere the dawn I should draw my last breath
And the sleep that I take be the long sleep of death,
Be near me, dear Mother, for dear Jesus' sake
When my soul on Eternity's shore shall awake.

A Prayer For Daily Neglects

Eternal Father, I offer Thee the Sacred Heart of Jesus, with all its love, all its sufferings and all its merits.

First -- To expiate all the sins I have committed this day and during all my life.

> *(Glory be to the Father and to the Son and the Holy Ghost; as it was in the beginning, is now, and ever shall be, world without end. Amen.)*

Second -- To purify the good I have done badly this day and during all my life.

> *(Glory Be to the Father...)*

Third -- To minister for the good I ought to have done, and that I have neglected this day and during all my life.

> *(Glory Be to the Father...)*

A poor Clare nun who had just died, appeared to her Abbess, who was praying for her, and said to her, "I went straight to Heaven, for, by means of this prayer, recited every evening, I paid all my debts."

INTRODUCTION

We begin the rosary with the Apostles' Creed. The Creed, as we have it today, goes back to Charlemagne (c. 800 A.D.). The roots of the Creed, however, go back to the apostles. Very likely, the Creed in embryo existed before the end of the first century and originated in Rome. Because of the special position of Rome, the entire West accepted it.

About 390 A.D. a priest of Aquileia, Rufinus (+410), wrote a commentary on what he called "The Belief of the Apostles." Hence the name "Apostles' Creed."

Rufinus said that the apostles composed the Creed before leaving each other to evangelize the world, so that there would be unity to their teaching. The last commission given them by Jesus was that they were to "go and make disciples of all nations, baptizing them in the name of the Father, and of the Son, and of the Holy Spirit..." (*Matt.* 28:19).

Consequently, the core of their Creed was the

three questions put to persons seeking baptism:

"Do you believe in God the Father Almighty?"
"Do you believe in Jesus Christ, the Son of God?"
"Do you believe in the Holy Spirit?"

By the third century this triple formula developed into the articles of the Creed. But the articles most amplified were those on Christ and the Holy Spirit, for the baptized were to follow Christ, and the Holy Spirit was the life of the Church into which they were baptized.

In the fourth century, the question-and-answer form gave way to declarative statements. And these eventually took the shape of the Creed, as we know it, under Charlemagne (c. 800 A.D.).

A Creed is necessary to define the Faith. A Christian must be able to stand up and say, "This is what I believe."

Equally important, a Christian must live the Faith, express it in works. "What good is it," asked James, "if someone says he has faith but does not have works?" (*Jas.* 2:14).

The apostles died for the Faith, for the truths incorporated in the Creed.

May we live that same Faith and die in it!

Teresa of Avila's last words were, "I die a daughter of the Church."

APOSTLES' CREED

I believe in God, the Father Almighty, Creator of Heaven and earth,

And in Jesus Christ, His only Son, Our Lord; Who was conceived by the Holy Spirit, born of the Virgin Mary, suffered under Pontius Pilate, was crucified, died, and was buried. He descended into Hell; the third day He arose again from the dead; He ascended into Heaven, sits at the right hand of God the Father Almighty; from thence He shall come to judge the living and the dead.

I believe in the Holy Spirit: the Holy Catholic Church; the communion of saints, the forgiveness of sins, the resurrection of the body, and life everlasting. Amen.

Chapter 1

"I believe in God, the Father Almighty, Creator of Heaven and earth"

Our Lady said, "The most beautiful prayer is the Creed," because "the most important thing is to believe." Belief is faith. Without faith it is impossible to please God. The Creed begins with an act of faith: "I believe."

Faith, however, is *more* than believing someone. When you say, "I believe him or her," you mean "I believe they are telling the truth; they are not lying." Faith is more than believing a lot of truths.

The Creed begins with the words "I believe *in* God." The preposition "in" is very important. For to believe *in* someone is more than believing someone. To believe someone means I know he or she is not lying. But to believe *in* someone means, "I know the person. I know I can trust him. Trust him absolutely, not only to tell the truth, but to do everything he says or promises he will do. I believe in him—that is, I have so much faith in him that I wouldn't hesitate to entrust him with my money or even my life."

Real faith is like that. It is to so believe in God that I would not hesitate to surrender my life to Him. When Jesus commanded Peter to walk on stormy waters, Peter took the dangerous risk—that was faith.

God is three Persons. To believe in God is to have faith in the Father, in the Son and in the Holy Spirit.

I believe in God, the Father Almighty, Creator of Heaven and earth.

The first act of faith in the Creed is to believe in God as Father. God is a Father, not only because He has a Son from all eternity, but also because in time He created everything that exists. He is Father because He is the Creator. He is Almighty because to create means to make something out of nothing. To make something out of nothing requires tremendous power—almighty power.

And what did the Father create? Heaven and earth. "I believe in God, the Father Almighty, Creator of Heaven and earth." So there are two heavens; the uncreated Heaven where the Father, the Son and the Holy Spirit dwell; and the created heavens where God put the angels.

Before the angels could get into the uncreated heavens, they had to prove their love of God, just as we must do. Some of them failed. They became devils or bad angels. For them Hell was created. Hell, you see, was never in the original creation of God; it was the result of the rebellion of some of the created angels. Thus Jesus spoke of Hell as "the eternal fire prepared for the devil and his angels." (*Matt.* 25:41).

To take the place of these fallen angels, God created man. That made the fallen angels unbelievably furious. So they attack us with leonine ferocity and seek to deprive us of the happiness they have lost. God permits this, because this gives us a chance to prove our love for Him and thus win the uncreated Heaven.

But because angels are so much more powerful than we are, God assigns a guardian angel to each one of us to balance off matters. These guardian angels protect us and guard us in life's journey. They love us and help us more than we realize. Each one of us should cultivate great devotion to his own guardian angel.

However, before God created man, He had to clear up the chaos created by the rebellion of the fallen angels. There was darkness over the face of the earth; it was a wasteland! So God made light, separated the waters above the heavens from the waters on the earth, then the earth waters from the dry land which He covered with grass and plants.

Once God had made the earth habitable again, He then furnished it with lights (the sun, the moon, the stars), with birds and fish, with animals and, as a crowning touch, with man.

God took special care with man. He fashioned him out of the clay of the ground; then He blew into his nostrils the breath of life—to show that man had a little bit of earth in himself and a little bit of God.

From this man God drew woman, for woman was to be less earthy than man. He drew her from man's side—not from his head, for she was not to dominate him; nor from his feet for he was not to dominate her; but from his side, because she was to be closest to his heart and to stand beside him and walk side by side with him down the journey of life.

How truly a Father is God! How good a Father! The mystic Eileen George always speaks of God the Father as "Daddy-God." How true that is! God's relationship to us is more than that of Creator to creature; He is Daddy, Papa, Abba, and we are His children.

What a wonderful home He has built for us! For a roof, the skies, the clouds, the sun, the moon, the stars; for a floor, the green grass, the flowers of the field, running brooks and waving trees. How lavishly He has provided for us: He has given us the earth and the abundance thereof.

In the beginning, He made this world a paradise. For Daddy-God created us for happiness. He wants us to be happy. But we are free. So often that's the rub! Like the fallen angels we too can rebel. We can turn paradise into a vale of tears, create our own hells.

But our Father, like most fathers, puts up with the antics of His wayward children with infinite patience. While there is life, He hopes! He so wants His children to be happy. And He sent His Son to point out to us the way to happiness. "Not everyone who says to me 'Lord, Lord' will enter the kingdom of Heaven, but only the one who does the will of my Father in Heaven." (*Matt.* 7:21). Doing the Father's will—it is that simple.

Chapter 2

"And in Jesus Christ, His only Son, Our Lord"

So God made man to fill up the thrones left vacant by the fall of the angels. He made man to His own image.

Since He is love, He created the sexes: God made man male and female. For love is relational: to love, one needs another.

But God is also one in three Persons. Therefore God made sex to be: (1) *unitive*, to help man and woman become one in marriage, as He is One; and (2) *creative*, the gateway of life, to help man and woman create the family, as He is a family of three Persons.

Now the God our Father is a happy God, so He gave man everything he needed to be ecstatically happy: a world that was a paradise and a woman who was a suitable partner for him—a woman with whom he could become one, to be fertile and multiply and fill the earth.

To keep this primeval happiness for himself and his children, God told the man not to eat the fruit of a tree. What God meant was, "Don't declare your independence of Me. Don't try to go it on your own, to set up your own standards. I made you, I know what is best for you. My Will, not yours, is the path to happiness."

That was all right with the man and the woman, for they had it so good. But an extraterrestrial being entered the scene—Satan, the leader of the fallen angels. He envied the man and the woman. And envy is an ugly sin: it is sadness over the good fortune of another, so much so that it seeks even to strip the other of his or her good fortune. That is precisely what Satan set out to do; that is why the author of Genesis pictured him as a slithering snake. And strange as it might seem, the first man and woman fell for his terrible lies. They disobeyed God. And their disobedience opened a veritable Pandora's box of evils.

They lost their intimacy with God: sanctifying grace. They lost their innocence and felt the sting of the flesh. The man and the woman were hurt in their essential roles. He could provide for his family now, only by the sweat of his brow; and she could bear children now, only in pain. And to end it all, they were to return to dust.

What was even worse is that the effects of their original sin of pride and disobedience was visited upon all their children. As children of a father who has gambled away his fortune are born penniless, so all of us children of the first man and woman enter this world without the wealth of grace, with a strong tendency to do what we want and not what God wants, and with a legacy of sickness, suffering and death.

This damage was so cosmic that no man could undo it. Like Humpty Dumpty, we were good eggs when we came from the hands of God; but like Humpty Dumpty, we had a great fall; and all the king's horses and all the king's men couldn't put Humpty Dumpty together again. The King Himself had to come. God the Father had to send His Son, the King of kings.

You see, the gravity of an offense is gauged by the dignity of the one offended. If I shoot at a target, no harm. If I shoot at my neighbor's chickens, well maybe I will be fined. But if I shoot at my neighbor, then that's a whole differ-ent story. You see, prescinding from motives, the object determines the gravity of the shooting.

Sin is an offense against God. God is Infinite. Consequently sin is infinite. The sin of our first parents, therefore, put us in a terrible quan-dary. Like a suicide, man was able to do what he could not undo. The reason for this is that the worth of an apology is gauged, unlike an offense, by the dignity of the one making the apology. A wife offended by her husband will not accept an apology from the children.

So that was the problem of our redemption. Man had incurred an infinite debt but, being only man, he didn't have a cent to pay it.

To heal this rift between God and man caused by sin, a God had to come Who could pay an infinite debt; and this God had to become a man, for man incurred the debt. At the same time this God-man had to be one single person, otherwise neither could act for the other.

This union of God and man in the second Person of the Trinity is what we mean by the Incarnation. This God-made man is Jesus Christ. Because He is God's only Son, Our Lord, He alone can be the Bridge between Heaven and earth. By His divinity, Jesus could touch the shores of Heaven; by His humanity, He could touch the shores of earth; and in the oneness of His personality, He could join Heaven and earth together—in Him justice and peace met and kissed. (*Ps.* 85:11). Thus we call Jesus our High Priest, our Supreme Pontiff (the word "pontiff" in Latin means "bridge-builder").

In this article of the Creed we say, "I believe in Jesus Christ, His only Son, Our Lord." Because Jesus Christ is the only Son of God, He is Our Lord. And He is truly Our Lord only if we are loyal to Him: obey, love, follow, fight for Him as soldiers do for their commander. Jesus did not say *discuss Me*, but *follow Me*. At baptism He does not ask are you interested in Me, but do you choose Me over Satan? "Do you renounce Satan?"

We have a double enemy, just as our first parents had: An enemy from within (the strong inner tendency of wanting to do what we want, instead of what God wants) and an enemy from without (Satan). At Medjugorje Our Lady warns us constantly about Satan. His hate for us has not abated since the beginning. "Your opponent the devil is prowling around like a roaring lion looking for someone to devour." (*1 Ptr.* 5:8). That is why St. Paul urges us to "put on the armor of God so that you may be able to stand firm against the tactics of the devil." (*Eph.* 6:11).

Our Lady has repeatedly told us what this armor is. First of all, it is fasting, on Wednesdays and Fridays. Fasting will counteract the inner tendency to egoism. Then to overcome the attacks of Satan, she tells us to use the sacraments and the sacramentals: daily Mass, when possible; monthly confession; the wearing of blessed objects (the brown scapular, etc.); and the rosary prayed daily. Without this armor, we shall be left naked to our enemies; with it, our enemies are powerless.

Chapter 3

"Who was conceived by the Holy Spirit, born of the Virgin Mary"

God the Father wanted His Son to enter this world like any other child, namely, through a family. And the Son wanted to be like us in all things but sin.

So from all eternity, the Father picked a woman to be the mother of His Son. In Eden He spoke of her: "I will put enmity between you and the woman, and between your offspring and hers." (*Gen.* 3:15). Then through Isaiah He prophesied: "...the virgin shall be with child, and bear a son, and shall name him Immanuel." (7:14). The woman would be a virgin mother!

Her name was Mary. To make her a worthy mother for His Son, God filled her with grace. "God the Father," wrote St. Louis de Montfort, "made an assemblage of all the waters and He named it the sea (*mare* in Latin means 'sea'). He made an assemblage of all His graces and called it Mary (*maria* is the Latin plural for seas)." (*True Devotion*, p. 14).

For her husband, and the foster-father of her Son, God picked a man named Joseph. He foreshadowed the role Joseph was to play by the story of Joseph in Egypt. (*Gen.* 37:50). Like that Joseph, he was to be provider for and protector of the holy family—no more! Thus "when Mary was betrothed to Joseph, but before they lived together, she was found with child through the Holy Spirit." (*Matt.* 1:18).

The first Adam came from God without the intervention of woman; the second Adam came from God without the intervention of man. The Son of God Who had a Father in Heaven would have none on earth; He Who had no mother in Heaven would have one on earth. So the Son of God "was conceived by the Holy Spirit."

How deeply the Holy Spirit loves Mary! From all eternity both God the Father and God the Son had produced a divine Person. The Holy Spirit only was barren. He became fruitful by Mary, whom He has espoused. It was with her, in her and of her that He produced His Masterpiece, which is God made man.

How indebted He feels toward her! For her consent to conceive of the Holy Spirit was freely and lovingly given to the Archangel Gabriel. At the very instant she gave it, the Holy Spirit made the Word of God flesh in her womb.

We celebrate this event of God entering into

the arena of history on March 25, Annunciation Day. So momentous was this happening that it split time in two: time before His coming is B.C. *before Christ;* and time after His coming is A.D. *in the year of Our Lord.* And we recall this glorious event three times a day with the ringing of church bells and the praying of the Angelus.

Because of His close relationship to Mary, the Holy Spirit specially favors all those who are close to her. Hence the importance of true devotion to Mary.

Because Mary conceived by the Holy Spirit, the Church in the *Confiteor* speaks of her as "ever-virgin." "Ever-virgin" means that Mary was a virgin *before, during* and *after* the birth of her Son, Jesus. Before His birth, for she conceived by the Holy Spirit. During His birth, for He issued from her womb in the cave at Bethlehem without breaking the seal of her virginity—as light passes through glass without breaking it. And after His birth, for Mary had no other children. As the burning bush that Moses saw was not consumed by the flames that engulfed it, so the Son of Mary—the flaming Sun of Justice— did not consume the virginity of His mother.

The "brothers of the Lord" spoken of in the gospels refer to relatives. Neither Hebrew nor Aramaic has any word for cousin. All relatives are called brothers. Thus nowhere are James,

Joses, Simon and Jude spoken of as children of Mary. The gospels imply Jesus was an only Son: the finding in the Temple does; so does the fact that Jesus on the cross entrusted His mother to John—an odd thing to do, to say the least, if she had had other sons.

When Jesus is spoken of as Mary's "firstborn" Son, it would be wrong to interpret this as meaning there was a second born. "Firstborn" is a technical term for the male who opened the womb and was specially consecrated to God. (*Ex.* 13:2, *Lk.* 2:23). "Firstborn" means one before whom there is no other; not one after whom came others.

Lastly, it would be just as wrong to take Matthew's statement "Joseph had not relations with her *until* she bore a Son, and he named Him Jesus" (1:25) and to interpret the word "until" as though Mary remained a virgin until the birth of Jesus but not afterwards. "Until" is concerned with what precedes, not with what follows. Actually, all Matthew meant was that Joseph was not the natural father of Jesus—the conception was a virginal one. That, too, is the sense of the Greek text.

Mary married, as we said, because God wanted Jesus to be born in a family, as every human being is. However, there was another reason: an unwed mother in those days would have posed problems not only for Mary, but also for Jesus.

Today, the world paradoxically tends to scorn virginity as unproductive and to abort the productivity of motherhood.

Mary was a virgin, yet a mother, as if to teach that the consecrated virginity of the religious life is and can be highly productive.

She was mother yet a virgin, as if to teach husbands and wives that there is a "planned parenthood" that is possible, yet not sinful—a sympto-thermic method—in lieu of the greatly sinful artificial contraception method.

Only God is the author of life, not we; He determines how life is to come into this world—normally by husband and wife. A virginal conception may awe us, but nothing is impossible with God. So we firmly believe that the Son of God "was conceived by the Holy Spirit, born of the Virgin Mary." Wonderful are the ways of God!

Chapter 4

"Suffered under Pontius Pilate, was crucified, died, and was buried"

All men are born to live; only one Man was born to die—Jesus Christ. That is why after saying "was born of the Virgin Mary," the Creed skips over all the rest of His life to its end: "suffered under Pontius Pilate, was crucified, died, and was buried."

St. Thomas said that one single drop of Jesus' blood could have saved the entire world: ". . .cleanse me in Thy blood/Of which a single drop for sinners spilt/Can purge the entire world of all its guilt." If one single drop would have sufficed, why the terrible suffering under Pontius Pilate and crucifixion?

The two beams of the cross tell us why.

The horizontal beam, like outstretched arms, tell us that Jesus died because He loved us so much. "No one has greater love than this, to lay down one's life for one's friends." (*Jn.* 15:13).

Someone said: "I asked Jesus how much He loved me."

Jesus answered: "This much"—and He stretched out His arms on the cross and died.

> *The trees and flowers all speak of*
>   *God's love,*
> *And the sky reveals it from above,*
> *But neither flowers nor clouds nor sun*
> *Can teach what His love for me has*
>   *done—as my crucifix!*

The vertical beam, like a dagger, proclaims how horrendous sin must be that killed the Son of God. The cross says, "This is sin: crucifixion."

He suffered under Pontius Pilate, for crucifixion was a Roman punishment.

Pontius Pilate was procurator of Judea from about 26 A.D. to 35 A.D. He was around the same age as Jesus—but a proud, aristocratic and autocratic man. His wife was Claudia Procula, the granddaughter of the Emperor Augustus. She was cultured, sophisticated, and pleaded in Jesus' behalf during His trial. (*Matt.* 27:19).

Pilate's chief concern was himself. His sole question was not "What is my duty?" but "How does this or that affect me?" All that the Jews wanted from Pilate was the death sentence for Jesus. But Jesus suffered much more because of the wicked weakness of Pontius Pilate.

Jesus was sent to Herod and humiliated by

that devious fox because of the wicked weakness of Pilate.

Jesus was put on the same level with the notorious criminal Barabbas, and Barabbas was preferred to Him, because of the wicked weakness of Pilate.

Jesus was scourged by the horrible lash, and was mocked as a king with a crown of piercing thorns, all because of the wicked weakness of Pilate.

Pilate tried to wash his hands of the whole affair, but saying it isn't so, doesn't make it so. Actions speak louder than words; thus the Creed says, "Suffered under Pontius Pilate."

(Pilate was removed from office in 36 A.D. and was banished to Vienne on the Rhone in southern France. Tradition has it that he, like Judas, ultimately committed suicide in Switzerland by drowning in the dismal lake on the summit of Mt. Pilatus overlooking Lake Lucerne.)

Jesus' cruel and brutal suffering under Pontius Pilate culminated in the even more painful death by crucifixion. Here the gospel writers maintain a discreet silence. Their accounts are so objective and unemotional that they resemble a medical or scientific report. "They crucified Him." That is all they say. But oh, so frightful and excruciating was death by crucifixion that it was reserved by Romans only for foreigners and slaves.

On the cross Jesus died like the God that He was—praying for His enemies and thinking only of others. So Godlike was He on the cross that Dismas, the thief, and Longinus, the centurion, both confessed Him to be the Son of God. Then when He died, even all Nature was disturbed. The sun darkened, the earth shuddered and shook, riving and rending rocks, the Temple veil was torn from top to bottom, and graves yielded their dead. As Shakespeare wrote: "When beggars die no comets are seen. . ./The heavens themselves blaze forth the death of princes."

Skeptics who would challenge the resurrection of Jesus often begin by denying that He really died. So the Creed adds, "suffered under Pontius Pilate, was crucified, died, and WAS BURIED." Only the dead are buried.

Longinus made sure Jesus was dead, by piercing His side with a lance. Pilate also confirmed this before granting Joseph of Arimathea permission to bury Jesus. Thus both friend and enemy testified to the actuality of Jesus' death.

And He was buried in a garden, as if to hint that the debt incurred in the garden of Eden had been paid.

His tomb, like Mary's womb, was a new one, untenanted by anyone else, so that later on no one could say someone else, besides Jesus, had arisen from the tomb.

The tomb had been hewn from rock. This meant it had but one entrance—and a guarded one at that! To steal the body was impossible.

To grasp the meaning of the passion and death of Jesus more deeply, the Church has highly indulgenced the beautiful devotion called the Way of the Cross.

It is very likely that the Way of the Cross owes its origin to the Mother of God. In the Revelations of St. Bridget, Our Lady said, "For all the time that I lived after the Ascension of my Son, I visited the places in which He suffered and showed His wonders. So rooted, too, was His Passion in my heart, that whether I ate or worked, it was ever as if fresh in memory" (p. 67).

Again Our Lady told St. Bridget, "Some years after the Ascension of my Son, I was one day much afflicted with a longing to rejoin my Son; then I beheld a radiant angel, such as I had before seen, who said to me: 'Thy Son, Who is Our Lord and God, sent me to announce to thee that the time is at hand when thou shalt come bodily to Him, to receive the crown prepared for thee.'"

She went on to tell St. Bridget that the angel disappeared and that she prepared herself for her departure by "going, as was my wont, to all the spots where my Son had suffered; and when one day my mind was absorbed in admiring contemplation of Divine Charity, my soul was filled therein with such exultation that it could not contain itself, and in that very consideration, my soul was loosed from the body."

Two beautiful thoughts, I think, are here. First, Mary died from love. As harp strings burst asunder with the music they throb to express, so Mary died of love. And secondly, she died while making the Stations of the Cross. And I like to believe that it was while contemplating the great love of Jesus shown on the cross of Calvary that her heart burst from love. In other words, I like to think that she died on Calvary just like her Son.

What happened was that the early Christians began to follow Mary's example. At first, some of the Christian women went with her to the way of Our Lord's cross. After her death, the Way of the Cross became the first place for Christian pilgrims to visit and to make. This gave rise to processions—always preceded with a cross at the head. Even today a cross-bearer leads our processions.

We should often make the Way of the Cross; at least every Friday, because reflection on the passion and death of Jesus can transform one's life.

Below is a true story of how the contemplation of Jesus on the cross actually changed the life of a noted British sculptor.

One day while strolling in her friend's garden, this artist noticed a cherry tree divided into three branches: two resembled arms extended toward Heaven and the third, bent slightly forward, suggested a head turned toward earth. "This tree," she thought, "might be transformed into a figure of Christ on the cross."

Her friend donated the tree. Her brother, tied to a makeshift cross, for minutes at a time, served as a model. She carved for months. Gradually, limb by limb, feature by feature, the body of the suffering man on the cross emerged. Resting before the fireplace on long winter evenings, she would gaze with awe on her suffering Jesus.

Before, Jesus on the cross meant little to her—just a religious symbol. But now, staring into His compassionate face, she found herself asking if all this were really true. Did He die on a cross? Did He love us so much? Is sin so terrible?

When her crucifix was finished, all were

impressed—but none so much as the sculptor herself. The long days and months she had spent meditating on the carving had changed her heart. Soon after, she became a Catholic.

Her name is Mrs. Clare Consuelo Sheridan, noted sculptor, cousin to Sir Winston Churchill—and witness to the transforming power that the contemplation of the crucifixion can have.

It still has that power. That is why the Church has so highly indulgenced the making of the Way of the Cross.

Chapter 5

"He descended into Hell, the third day He arose again from the dead"

This article of the Creed is beset with all kinds of difficulties. It was a Johnny-come-lately truth, inserted into the Creed about 570 A.D.

First, the word "descended" suggests a 3-story universe: the created heavens above, the earth in the center, and the abode of the dead below. Such a structural universe is hardly acceptable to modern man.

Then there is the word "Hell." Today "Hell" means the place of punishment for the damned. But it does not mean that in the Creed. The New Testament speaks of the Hell of the damned as "Gehenna" (*Matt.* 5:29-30; 10:28) or "Tartarus" (2 *Ptr.* 2:4). For Heaven, it uses expressions, like "Abraham's bosom" (*Lk.* 17:22) or "paradise" (*Lk.* 23:43).

"Hell" in the Creed refers to Hades (*Acts* 2:27, 31) or *Sheol*. For both Greeks and Jews, Hades or *Sheol* was the land of the dead—a grey, shadowy land having no light, no color, no joy, where its inhabitants moved like ghosts and were more non-being than being.

In saying Jesus descended into Hell, the Creed is stating two things.

First, it is saying that Jesus had really and truly died, that He had tasted death to the last drop. Thus Pope John Paul II said: "During the three (incomplete) days between the moment when He 'expired' (cf. *Mk.* 15:37) and the Resurrection, Jesus experienced the 'state of death,' that is, the separation of body and soul, as in the case of all people." (In the Creed for children's Masses, this phrase is put simply as "He descended to the dead"—that is, He really died.)

Secondly, this phrase "He descended into Hell" is saying that the redemption effected by Jesus extended to all peoples—even to those who have lived and died before Christ. The Holy Father, John Paul II, in commenting on this passage from the Epistle of Peter, "He went to preach to the spirits in prison (*1 Ptr.* 3:19), said, "This seems to indicate metaphorically the extension of Christ's salvation to the just men and women who had died before Him." (1/11/89).

Be that as it may, the statement was meant to give us hope. Hell, you know, is abandonment by God; it is the absence of God. On a retreat given by Eileen George, she gave this graphic description of the essential pain of Hell.

"Many times in my ministry," she said, "I hear complaints—physical, spiritual—whatever. But the most common complaint, the one I hear so often is, 'God has abandoned me.' 'He has left me.' 'I don't want to pray.' 'I don't feel like praying.' 'He doesn't hear me.' 'He never answers my prayers.' 'If He is around, why has He done this to me?'

"Everytime I hear this complaint, 'God has abandoned me,' I think of the teaching on Hell. So I'm going to share with you a vision or dream of mine on Hell, not to frighten you, but to teach you a lesson, as I have to learn a lesson.

"I once had a dream...I saw God my Father. He said to me, 'Hold My hand, child, I want to take you someplace.' So I held the Father's hand, and He took me to these huge gates. The gates weren't made out of iron or wood or any material I had ever seen. And the Father freed Himself from me and said, 'You must enter. I cannot go in this place.' I was baffled, but I obeyed...The Father freed His hand from me, and I pushed my way through these gates. I heard the big clank behind me—the doors shut.

"It was a place of darkness, yet light, yet

not according to our light. It was a place of dampness, a place of terrible odors. There was nothing living, no signs of life: no grass, no birds, no chirping in the trees for there were no trees—no signs of life whatsoever. And I began to feel a little frightened. I smelled the horrible aroma, but it wasn't coming from the level I was on (even in Hell—this was the first level—there are many levels going down into Hell according to the Father's justice). I knew the aroma, the nauseous smell of burnt flesh, coming from another level.

"It was a terrible place. I wanted to run and get out of there, because a terrible pain was gripping inside my stomach. It seemed like I was going to die. I had to get out of this place (I have cancer and I suffer a lot—sometimes when I suffer, I think I'm going to lose my mind). I had to get out of this place, because this place was terrible and the pain was excruciating—something I have never before experienced. When I tried to move, my feet were like in cement.

"Finally, I saw two creatures. They were like a charcoal stump, but no leaves, no sign of life. They were naked, but I couldn't tell if they were man or woman. Their hair was long and dark. And finally, when my feet were free, I saw these people look toward me, having the most hideous faces I have ever seen. Their eye sockets were like eggs, and fire was going up inside the eyeballs, not coming out.

"But even all that was not as bad as the pain I felt inside of me. It was by far the most excruciating pain I have ever had.

"Finally, I reached the door and I fell outside the door at the Father-God's feet. The pain was gone! I realized as I looked up into my Father's eyes that this pain was the absence of Daddy-God in that place.

"So the greatest pain in Hell is the absence of God. It was an excruciating pain, but as soon as I was outside the gate before the Father, the pain was gone.

"So, if that was such an excruciating pain, don't come to me and say, 'God has abandoned me.' On earth God never abandons us. He never moves away from us. It is we who move away from Him. But He never abandons us here."

Now death is also an abandonment—an abandonment by everyone. It is absolute loneliness. For one dies alone. One goes to the grave alone. That is why the Old Testament had only one word for Hell and death: the word *Sheol*. In the sense of abandonment, the Old Testament regarded Hell and death as identical.

But Jesus descended to the dead precisely to attack this abandonment. The dead are now no longer alone. He is there. Elizabeth Kubler-Ross in the Foreword to Dr. Moody's *Life after Life* has written:

> "...the dying patient continues to have a conscious awareness of his environment after being pronounced clinically dead.
>
> "All of these patients have experienced a floating out of their physical bodies, associated with a great sense of peace and wholeness. Most were aware of *another person* who helped them in their transition to another plane of existence."

Christ awaits the dying. He is Love. He is Life. He is a Person. If a little child gets lost in the woods in the dark of night, terror grips its tiny heart. And no reasoning, nothing will dispel this terror except another person, a mother or dad, finding the child and picking up and hugging the child. Only that will drive away the terror. In the agony in the garden, Jesus wanted only one thing: company. Thus in answer to His prayer, the Father sent another person: an angel to strengthen Him. (*Lk.* 22:43).

So the terrible fear that can arise from a sense of abandonment at the time of death is gone, because Jesus had descended to the dead. His descent has swallowed up death in victory. Thus St. Paul could cry out: "Where, O death, is your victory? Where, O death is your sting?" (*1 Cor.* 15:55). "The sting of death is sin," because only sin can shut out Christ; and to die without Christ makes abandonment eternal—which is Hell or the second death. (*Rev.* 20:14).

So, "He descended into Hell" (to the dead) is a statement of hope. It not only tells us death has been robbed of its terror, but also that we can cope with those periods in life when we say, "God has abandoned me."

Holy Saturday followed Good Friday. For one brief moment, God was "dead"—was buried in a tomb, absent from the world He had made. He walked the earth no longer. He no longer spoke. There was only silence—the silence of the tomb. He had descended to the dead—He had "left" the world. How bleak it was on that first Holy Saturday! Mary's seventh sorrow was His burial. Mary Magdalene wept at His tomb. On that first Easter, the two disciples on the road to Emmaus had lost hope. (*Lk.* 24:21).

So often, God may seem dead in our lives: we do not feel God the way we think we should. We may even say, "God has abandoned me." How foolish! God never abandons us. He may be silent. He may seem "dead." But He lives— for "the third day He arose again from the dead!" He arose to raise us up after our periods of desolation and abandonment. We, too, must descend to the dead, for gold is tried by fire. And if we are faithful during our periods of trial, a resurrection to a new and better life will inevitably follow as surely as Easter Sunday followed the first Holy Saturday.

He descended to the dead to rob death of its terror and to carry us over the "Hell" periods of life—to give us hope.

Chapter 6

"He ascended into Heaven, sitteth at the right hand of God the Father Almighty"

Talk of the ascension, together with the descent into Hell, conjures up the picture of a 3-story universe. We said such a universe is hardly acceptable to modern man. "Above," and "below"—the world is everywhere, and it is governed everywhere by the same physical laws. It is no 3-story structure.

The ideas "above" and "below" ("ascended" and "descended") are really relative terms depending upon where one is standing. We have no absolute point of reference here, so we can hardly speak of "above" and "below"—or, for that matter, of "left" and "right."

No one will argue with these observations about a 3-story world. But was such a conception ever really intended in these articles of the Creed about Our Lord's descent into Hell and His ascension into Heaven? The imagery is there, but His "going up" or "going down" was not the basic element in those articles.

As we saw Christ's descent into Hell did not refer to any outer depths of the cosmos—such movement was not necessary. Rather the Creed is touching upon one of the deepest dimensions of human existence—the Hell of absolute loneliness, especially at death, deep down within the heart of man. Similarly, Christ's ascent into Heaven touches upon the opposite dimension of human existence—the highest exaltation to which man can rise by contact with God the Father, Heaven; and through contact with God with all other men.

Hell is of man's own making; but Heaven is a supernatural gift of God, a grace. Heaven is not to be understood as an everlasting place above the world. Heaven is where Christ is— where God and man in Christ meet with God the Father. Heaven and the ascension of Christ, therefore, are inseparably connected.

Heaven is the future of mankind. It was closed to man as long as man was left to himself. But the conjunction of God and man in Jesus, and His death—when He passed over from this life and "ascended into Heaven" to life with God His Father beyond this life—opened it.

In the preaching of Jesus and the apostles, it looked as if the end of the world was going to be soon—in the lifetime of the apostles. Perhaps this was so because Jesus' resurrection and ascension were the final merging of man with God—not just in Jesus, but in Jesus with the Father—a process which made an everlasting existence of happiness possible for man. It was the crossing of the frontier of death, opening up the future dimension of mankind—a future which in fact has already begun. Hence the idea that the end was soon—the imminent eschatology of the gospels.

By ascending into Heaven, Jesus broke all the bonds of the limitations imposed upon Himself by His humanity. The phrase "He sits at the right hand of God, the Father Almighty" means that He shares the Father's almighty power, so that now He is able to fill all things (*Eph.* 4:10). He is able now to act like the God that He is. He can send His Spirit upon the Church. He can intercede for us. He is now the Door (*Jn.* 10:4), the Mediator (*1 Tim.* 2:5) between man and the Father. He can so help us, that one day we too shall "ascend into Heaven"—be united forever with God His Father.

His ascension into Heaven, therefore, is not so much a change of place as of presence. Louis Evely wrote that in order to celebrate the ascension of Our Lord, "it is first of all necessary to understand the radical difference between a disappearance and a departure. A departure causes an absence; a disappearance inaugurates a hidden presence."

When Our Lord ascended into Heaven, He did not depart from us; He did not leave us orphans. "I am with you always, until the end of the age." (*Matt.* 28:20). As the Son of God did not leave His Father in Heaven by becoming man, so He does not leave us here on earth by ascending into Heaven.

He ascended not merely to glorify and exalt His humanity more fully, but also to be able to become more related to each one of us than ever before. And He can, because He sits at the right hand of the Father—shares His almighty power. Thus after the ascension St. Mark writes: "So the Lord Jesus. . .was taken up into Heaven and took His seat at the right hand of God." And because He was there, the right hand Man of the Father, He was able to empower the apostles to evangelize the world. Thus St. Mark continues: "But they went forth and preached everywhere, while the Lord worked with them and confirmed the Word through accompanying signs." (*Mk.* 16:19-20).

Again, what joy this article of the Creed should bring to us! Our Lord has disappeared, but not departed. Now He is able to be present to each one of us in a far better way than was ever possible in His bodily form—in prayer and in action, in the sacraments and in our neighbor. He is now everywhere—everywhere for us! Sitting at the right hand of His Father, "He lives forever to make intercession for us." (*Heb.* 7:25).

He ascended into Heaven, to exalt us all to the right hand of the Father, to the eternal union with Him, which is Heaven.

Chapter 7

"From thence He shall come to judge the living and the dead"

This article of the Creed contains two truths: first, the coming of Jesus—"from thence He shall come" (the Second Coming or Parousia); and secondly, His coming to judge the living and the dead—the dead of past generations and those living at the Second Coming. (*2 Tim.* 4:1; *1 Thess.* 4:17).

That Jesus will come again, two angels told the apostles after the ascension of Our Lord. "Men of Galilee," they said, "why are you standing there looking at the sky? This Jesus Who has been taken up from you into Heaven will return . . ." (*Acts* 1:11; 3:19-21). The Second Coming was an essential part of early Christian preaching.

That this same Jesus will judge the living and the dead was preached by both Peter and Paul. (*Acts* 10:42; 17:31). Jesus often taught of a judgment, especially in His parables. Failure to use one's talent is condemned (*Matt.* 25:14-30); failure to help one in need is severely judged. (*Matt.* 25:31-46). In the parable of Dives and Lazarus, Dives is in torment not for what he did, but for what he did not do for one in need. (*Lk.* 16:19-31).

Now the Second Coming of Jesus is generally viewed as marking the end of the world.

How do you imagine the end of the world? Do you think God will come down from above at the end of time, destroy this world, then take us all to paradise? Or do you think He invites us now to construct a new world with His help? Did He not teach us to pray, "Thy Kingdom come on earth as it is in Heaven"? Will the end of the world be a disaster or a completion? Will God end the world when He thinks He has put up with enough or will the world only end when it is complete? Does human effort play any part in God's plan?

At Medjugorje Our Lady has been inviting us to help her bring the world back to God, to help make the world a family, like the one she has created among the five villages of the parish of St. James at Medjugorje.

There are movements afoot in the world today to feed the hungry of the world, to liberate the oppressed, to make the world a better place in which to live. Christians must never look askance at these efforts nor stand aloof from them. Heralds of the gospel must not be Cassandras. Rather they should work along with all others seeking to humanize the planet.

Christ did not come to condemn the world but to save it. He has made us salt, light, and leaven to transform it. We must work to end selfishness, greed and pride. We must help create a new people, filled with love, humility, generosity. We must pray for a new Pentecost of fire, grace and light to renew the Church. We must pray that God send forth His Spirit to renew the face of the earth, so that the end of the world will not be a disaster, but a completion.

We must work and pray that His Kingdom come on earth as it is in Heaven, so that in the end Christ might present to His Father "an eternal and universal Kingdom, a Kingdom of truth and life, a Kingdom of holiness and grace, a Kingdom of justice, love and peace" (Preface of Christ the King).

As the priest at every Mass takes the bread "which human hands have made," and transforms it into the Body of Christ, similarly by the Spirit and our efforts, the world must be so renewed that at the end Christ will be able to say to us, "Come and live here forever. This is the Kingdom prepared for you from the foundation of the world." (*Matt.* 25:34).

*   *   *

So much for the end of the world. It will be more profitable to meditate on the Second Coming that will signal the end of the world.

In the first place, the fact of the Second Coming tells us that history is linear, not cyclic; that is, that history is going forward in a straight line toward a very definite goal.

To the pagans history was cyclic, a merry-go-round, a series of events going around in circles, like the seasons, endlessly repetitive without variation. That explains why one of the hallmarks of paganism and atheism is ennui, boredom. If you had to drive your car in circles, you would be driven mad. Life without purpose is maddening, like digging postholes and filling them up again.

G. K. Chesterton in his *Ballad of the White Horse* has brilliantly contrasted the joy of Christianity with the lassitude of paganism. The Ballad is about the invasion of the then Christian England by the pagan Danes under Guthrum. Chesterton depicts the Christians under Alfred the Great as men "shaken with the joy of giants"—for you can't have a cause and no joy, nor a faith and no hope. In contrast, the pagan Danes are men who see "only with heavy eyes." Guthrum, their leader, sits before the fire "with a smile carved on his lips." The pagans know not how to laugh, for "their gods were sadder than the sea."

Because we believe that "He shall come," history for the Christian is linear. Life is not an aimless, purposeless journey, going nowhere. There is a goal, there is purpose: life does lead somewhere. So life can be a royal road to romance as it was for the saints. To throw a bowling ball down an alley with no pins is no fun. However, put pins at the end of the alley, give purpose to throwing the ball, and it becomes an enjoyable game—fun. So life without purpose bores; with purpose, life is worth living.

That "He shall come to judge the living and the dead" tells us not only is life going somewhere, but that in the end Jesus will have the last word. Good, not evil, will win out in the end. So persevere. Mary at Fatima said the same thing: "In the end my Immaculate Heart will triumph."

Finally, "that He will come" need not be seen as a future event. Did not Jesus say, "Whoever loves Me will keep My word, and My Father will love him, and We will come to him and make our dwelling with him" (*Jn.* 14:23)? If we go to Jesus *now*, Jesus will come to us now. If we strive to know Him now by daily reading the gospels, He will know us then when He comes. "When you turn back to Him with all your heart, to do what is right before Him; then He will turn back to you, and no longer hide His face from you." (*Tob.* 13:6).

* * *

Now, our present decisions will determine how the world ends or shapes up. That is why when He comes, He will come to judge. No one can escape giving an account of the way he has lived his life. Every man will be judged according to his works.

But, you may wonder, if God is a Father, a God of mercy, why a judgment? Because we are free. To be free means to be responsible. To be responsible means to be answerable— answerable to someone. The Creed tells us this Someone is Jesus. And He has every right to judge us, because He knows our frame: He lived our life and knows what it means to be human; and because He died for us to win the graces whose acceptance or rejection will determine our judgment.

The early Church put the emphasis in this

article of the Creed on the word "He"—"HE shall come to judge the living and the dead." For the early Christians, this article was a note of hope, of joy! It said to them, "Think of it, our judge is not going to be a someone far off, distant, unfeeling, concerned only with condemning us, but a Someone Who is near to us, dear to us, our Brother, Who loves us and Who died for us—a real and true Friend! In a word, the cards are stacked in our favor." So the early Christians eagerly awaited the judgment. They cried out, "Marana, tha"—"Lord, come!" (*1 Cor.* 16:22; *Rev.* 22:20).

But in the Middle Ages, emphasis shifted from the joy and hope of religion to morality. So the emphasis in the Creed was put on the word "judge"—"He will come to JUDGE the living and the dead." The Judgment was seen as a terrifying event: "A Day of Wrath" *(Dies Irae)*— toward which man looked with fear and dread.

The early Christians were closer to the truth. This article of the Creed was meant to give us hope. It does not say—as one might expect— that God, the Almighty, the Infinite, the Unknown, the Eternal One will judge us. No, on the contrary, judgment is handed over to One Who, as Man, is our Brother, Who loves us, Who died for us. To One Who is not ignorant of our life but was like us in all things, but sin. To One Who is not a stranger out to condemn us, but One Whose judgment is meant to be a welcome.

So at every Mass, right after the Our Father, we pray: "Deliver us, Lord, from every evil...from sin and...from all anxiety *as we wait in joyful hope for the coming of our Saviour, Jesus Christ.*"

For if we strive to live without sin and anxiety, the judgment will most certainly be a blessing, not a condemnation but a welcome: "Come, you who are blessed by My Father. Inherit the Kingdom prepared for you from the foundation of the world." (*Matt.* 25:34).

Chapter 8

"I believe in the Holy Spirit: the Holy, Catholic Church; the Communion of Saints, the forgiveness of sins; the resurrection of the body and life everlasting"

As you know from the sign of the cross, the Catholic profession of faith is always Trinitarian: a belief in the Father, the Son and the Holy Spirit. In the Creed the entire last section deals with the Holy Spirit. All the last articles of the Creed relate to the Holy Spirit—to Him as Gift to the Church.

We must not divide the last articles of the Creed as though each one was separate from the other. We should not say, "I believe in the Holy Spirit"—period. Then "I believe in the Holy, Catholic Church"—period. No. We should rather say, "I believe in the Holy Spirit"—colon: "the Holy, Catholic Church"—semicolon; and so on to the end, as in this chapter heading.

The reason for this is that the Church—its holiness, its catholicity, its communion of saints, its power to forgive sins, the resurrection of the body, life everlasting—all these are the great works *(magnalia Dei)* of the Holy Spirit. We ought to recite this section of the Creed in amazement, wonder, joy, excitement.

The first work of the Spirit of God is to effect unity. He makes the Father and the Son one. Likewise, He also makes those who receive Him one body—the Church. The Church is conceived by the Holy Spirit. She is His great work.

And He works through her in two ways: by making the Church one and by sanctifying all who come to her. In other words, His work is that of unification and conversion. The Creed expresses this by the articles "the communion of saints," and "the forgiveness of sins."

Originally, the communion of saints referred not to persons (saints) but to the Holy Eucharist given to the Church by Christ. But the Holy Eucharist is the work of the Holy Spirit. Just before the consecration at Mass we pray: "Let Your Spirit come upon these gifts to make them holy, so that they may become for us the Body and Blood of Our Lord, Jesus Christ." *(Euch. Pr.* II). As the Holy Spirit came upon Mary and the Word was made flesh, so He comes upon the bread and wine that they may become the Body and Blood of Christ.

The Holy Spirit brings the risen Christ to our altars to create unity: make all eucharistic worshippers one, and all the churches over all the earth one Church. Thus after the consecration we pray: "May all of us who share in the Body and Blood of Christ be brought together in unity by the Holy Spirit." (*Euch. Pr.* II).

Love is the bond of unity. Love comes only through the Sacrament of Love (Holy Communion) and the God of Love (the Holy Spirit). At Mass, before the consecration, the priest holds his hands over the gifts of bread and wine and prays that the Holy Spirit change them into the physical body of Christ. After the consecration, the priest extends his hands over the assembly of worshippers and prays that the same Holy Spirit, through an infusion of love, change all those who receive Holy Communion into a community of love, the mystical body of Christ, the Church. Thus St. Augustine could say: "The Church makes the Eucharist, but the Eucharist makes the Church."

You can understand now why Our Lady at Medjugorje told Jelena: "Before Mass it is necessary to pray to the Holy Spirit." (11:83).

Soon Holy Communion was broadened to include the persons themselves who were united together and sanctified by it—a Communion of Saints.

Later, since love is stronger than death, a cosmic dimension was added. The Communion of

Saints was extended beyond the frontier of death. All who had received the one Spirit and His gifts remained one even after death. And because of this union, there can be a communion, a sharing, of spiritual gifts among the saints in Heaven, in Purgatory and on earth.

The real atheist is not somebody who says there is no God, but the person who says there is a God but does not believe He can change the world into a community of loving persons.

The Holy Spirit starts this change at baptism. As the Spirit hovered over the waters at creation and brought cosmos out of chaos, a beautiful world out of a wasteland, so the same Spirit hovers over the waters of baptism and changes one into a new creature whom the Father greets with joyful cry, "This is My beloved son."

At first, baptism was the great sacrament of "the forgiveness of sins." It was the time not only when an inner transformation took place, but also a visible one. At baptism the candidate made both a profession of faith by reciting the Creed and a declaration of conversion by renouncing the devil and all his works and pomps; namely, anything that divides the Church, like hate, dissension, discord.

Only gradually, and through painful experience, did people come to learn that even baptized Christians needed the forgiveness of sins. So the sacrament of reconciliation came to the foreground and baptism receded to the background, as the beginning of life rather than the expression of an active conversion. Even today, we speak of "born again" Christians. The fact is some drift so far away from their beginnings, their original commitment at baptism, that they need to begin again.

So the core element of the Church is not so much the people composing her as the Holy Spirit dwelling in her and working in and through her: making the people a Church—a community of loving persons through the Eucharist, baptism and the sacrament of reconciliation.

In Scripture the Holy Spirit came upon the Church always in answer to prayer. (*Acts* 1:14; 4:31). Therefore, the Mother of God told Jelena: "Begin each day by calling on the Holy Spirit. The most important thing is to pray to the Holy Spirit." Why? Because "when the Holy Spirit descends on earth, everything becomes clear, everything is transformed" (*Advent* 1983).

Earnestly, then, we must pray: "Come, Holy Spirit, fill our hearts with your love and renew the face of the earth."

Chapter 9

"The Holy, Catholic Church"

In the last article, we got a glimpse of the true nature of the Church. It is essentially the work of the Holy Spirit. It is the place where He manifests Himself through His works of unification and conversion. It is the instrument whereby He operates powerfully in history: through the communion of saints (the Eucharist) and the forgiveness of sins (baptism and reconciliation)—the framework of the Church.

If we understand this, we can resolve two problems about the Church posed by the words "holy" and "catholic."

First, we call the Church "holy." But if we look at it, from our everyday experience, we see the Church is anything but holy. Vatican Council II spoke of the sinful Church—the Church always needing to be reformed.

I remember an old professor of Church History in the seminary, who always seemed to make it a point to highlight the seamy side of the Church. At first we used to wonder why. Then one day he explained: "I don't want you ever to be scandalized by what you may run into in the Church. What has happened in the past can very likely happen in the future. The human element with all its imperfections will always be in the Church. But remember, the Church has a divine element—the Holy Spirit. He is the soul of the Church. And for that reason the gates of Hell—be they persecution or the scandal of error or immorality—will never prevail against her.

When the Creed calls the Church "holy," it is not referring to the holiness of her human element, the people, but to the divine element, the Holy Spirit, who through the sacraments bestows holiness on the unholy. The Church is holy because her Spouse is holy—the Holy Spirit. The Church is holy, because her Spouse makes her children a holy people—yes, even raises some of them to be canonized saints.

What a wonderful thing this is that God does not shun us because we are not holy! We tend to equate holiness with the shunning of the evil-doers and their destruction. Yet Jesus would not let James and John rain down fire on the unworthy. (*Lk.* 9:55). Nor did He let the zealous uproot the weeds growing with the wheat. (*Matt.* 13:30). True holiness mingles with the unholy. Thus Jesus mingled with sinners, ate with them, talked to them, was crucified between them. True holiness does not separate itself from sinners, but seeks them. True holiness does not condemn sinners, but strives to save them.

Hence the Church, which is truly holy because the Holy Spirit dwells in her, plunges into human wretchedness. She does not stay afar off from leprous sinners but touches them to cleanse them; she does not remain aloof from the fallen, but stoops down to raise them up. True holiness is love—for the Holy Spirit is Love—Love reaching out to lift up the down and out.

How comforting is this holiness of the Church! Don't we all need forgiveness, understanding and love? Isn't it wonderful that the Holy Spirit through His Church gives us a home, gives us hope, gives us love—to give us in the end eternal life?

Secondly, we call the Church "catholic." And we wonder about that too. "Catholic" means unity everywhere. But everywhere we see hate, division, dissent. We baptize children and make them sons of God, but often we are hard put to find His family in which to put His sons?

So often His Church is filled with so much prejudice, hate, selfishness, division. The seamless garment of Christ is torn to shreds by hundreds of other churches, all claiming to be the Church of Christ. Even the true Church of Christ becomes a stumbling-block to many who see her only as an institution concerned about the things of this world. And bitterly, they criticize her.

The Holy Spirit's work is to convert the world, to bear witness through the church community of God's love for the world. It does this through her catholicity: unity over all the world.

The extrinsic means of this unity is the episcopal structure created by the sacrament of Orders. The local church must be in communion with her Bishop and all Bishops throughout the world must be in communion with each other and the Bishop of Rome, the Pope.

The intrinsic means of this unity is love. Vatican Council II defined the Church as "a kind of sacrament or sign of intimate union with God, and of the unity of all mankind." (*Const. on Ch.* #1). What is this sacrament or sign? It is a community of people who deeply love one another. And why is this a sacrament or sign? Because such unity is only possible because of the presence of God. "Where two or three are gathered together in My name, there am I in the midst of them." (*Matt.* 18:20).

Whenever and wherever somebody sees two or three persons who really love one another, he is seeing God—God is being revealed. Love like that drew the pagans to the Church. "See how these Christians love one another." Love like that is "a sign of intimate union with God"—a sign meant to bring about the unity of all mankind, true catholicity.

We must be on guard lest we turn the Church into a conservatory for pious souls. Salt is meant to be taken out of the salt-cellar. **Every Mass closes with the commission to every Catholic to go out into the world and love the Lord by serving others.** To be baptized is to be commissioned to evangelize the world.

The very word "catholic" means universal. Hence the limits of the Church are the entire world—all nations. The Catholic community must be no narrower than the human race.

Only by saving others do we save ourselves. When we stand before God, He will ask us, "Where are the others? The rest?" It will be of little consequence if we have preserved our talent intact by burying it. The man who buried his talent lost it. (*Matt.* 25:28). When a saint was asked why he wished to leave home and go on the foreign missions, he answered, "I don't want to go to Heaven alone."

Chapter 10

*"The resurrection of the body,
and life everlasting"*

It is good to put these last two articles of the
Creed together, for the simple reason that too
often life everlasting is conceived as anything
but human. Life everlasting is viewed by some
as an anemic kind of existence in which we have
to leave everything we have ever loved or en-
joyed on this earth.

The resurrection of the body corrects this de-
lusion. It tells us that we are to be restored whole
and entire, with all our human hopes and dreams,
joys and human affections. The resurrection of
the body means our supernatural happiness will
also be a human happiness. The loves of this
earth that were so good will be there in life everlasting and our loved ones too.

This article of the Creed was put there in re-
sponse to the attacks of some heresies on the
body.

We must remember that the Bible seldom divides man into body and soul. The Bible speaks

simply of the "resurrection of the dead"—of the whole man, not of half of him. (*Matt.* 22:31; *Acts* 17:32; *1 Cor.* 15:12).

The division of man into body and soul was a Greek concept. The ancient Greeks believed the soul alone was immortal, that it could fend for itself without the body, that the body was a drag on the soul. Plato, Epictetus, Seneca despised the body as the prison of the soul. They thought and taught that man would be better off without it. Sometimes Solomon is accused of echoing this dualism that pronounces matter evil. "For the corruptible body burdens the soul and the earthen shelter weighs down the mind that has many concerns." (*Wis.* 9:15). All Solomon is saying is that the earthbound body is a drag on the heavenward aspirations of the soul.

Plato's dualism, however, did filter into Christianity by way of Gnosticism in the second century. Gnostics taught that the body was evil. Therefore suicide is good, for it obliterates the body and liberates the soul. Marriage also is bad, for it propagates bodies. Later, Manichaeism peddled the same errors.

To counteract this way of thinking, the article "resurrection of the body" was formulated in the Creed. It taught that man is not a dichotomy, but a whole person; that all of man was redeemed by Christ, not just his soul; and that all of us will rise up from the dead, that you will still be you and I will still be me.

At Mass the resurrection is beautifully symbolized. After we recite the Lamb of God three times, the priest breaks the host into three pieces. One piece he drops into the chalice wine, the bread (His Body) commingles with the wine (His Blood), to denote the resurrection of Christ. This same resurrection Christ also promises to all of us who eat this Bread and drink this Blood worthily. "Whoever eats My flesh and drinks My blood has eternal life, and I will raise him on the last day." (*Jn.* 6:54).

If our bodies are to be raised up, if our flesh is to be immortalized as is our soul, then we have a compelling reason to be pure and chaste, to respect our bodies.

A further reason to act chastely is the thought of everlasting life. "What profit would there be for one to gain the whole world and forfeit his life?" (*Matt.* 17:25)—his everlasting life! Shakespeare put it so well. "What win I if I gain the thing I seek?/A dream, a breath, a froth of fleeting joy:/Who buys a minute's mirth to wail a week?/Or sells eternity to get a toy?/For one sweet grape who will the vine destroy?" *(The Rape of Lucrece).*

The Broadway play, *Brigadoon,* was based on a fanciful story. The minister of the Scottish town, trying to protect his flock from the deadly contagion of the world, prevailed upon God to work a miracle. The good Dominie obtained that the townsfolk awake only once every hundred years. In this way, he thought, his flock would never be harmed by the aberrations of each century.

When the townsfolk of Brigadoon awoke for their single day of life in the twentieth century, Tommy Albright, a wealthy New Yorker hunting in Scotland, happened to stroll into the village. He fell in love at first sight with Fiona Mac-Laren. She agreed to marry Tommy if he would renounce his former life forever. Mr. Lundie, the kindly Dominie of Brigadoon, advised Tommy: "It is usually the hardest thing in the world to give everything, but it is the only way to get everything." Tommy gave everything and found everything: unending happiness in Brigadoon with Fiona.

Eternity—Heaven or Hell—it stands before us. It is ours to choose. "I set before you life and death...Choose life"—everlasting life! (*Deut.* 30:19).

To get everything—life everlasting—give everything.

Life Everlasting in Catechetics

A long time ago when I was a young priest, an old priest showed me how to diagram Life Everlasting in catechetics. I like it. So I share it with you. See the description below and the diagram on the next page.

1. Man is born to die as the bird is born to fly.

2. Death is the separation of soul from body.

3. The body returns to the dust from which it was made. The soul is promptly judged. This judgment is the Particular Judgment: the soul judges itself. It assigns itself to— Heaven (love without pain), Purgatory (love with pain), or Hell (pain without love), depending on the state it is in.

4. At the end of the world, there will be a General Resurrection of the Dead: body and soul will be reunited; the General Judgment will follow, to justify God's ways with men. Time will be no more. There will be only Heaven and Hell and Eternity.

①
Death

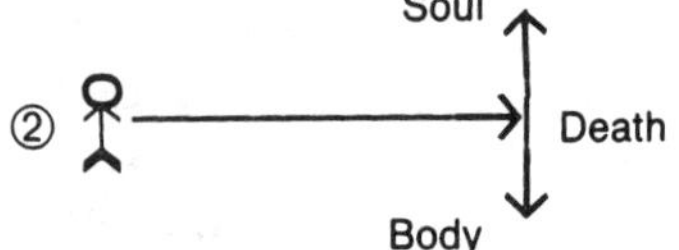
②
Soul
Death
Body

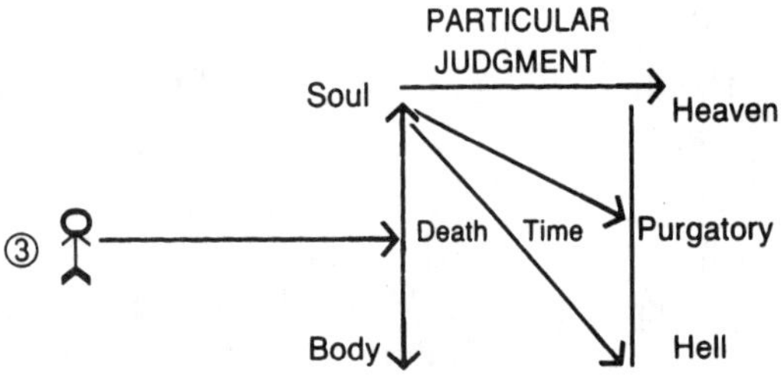
PARTICULAR
JUDGMENT
Soul
Heaven
③
Death
Time
Purgatory
Body
Hell

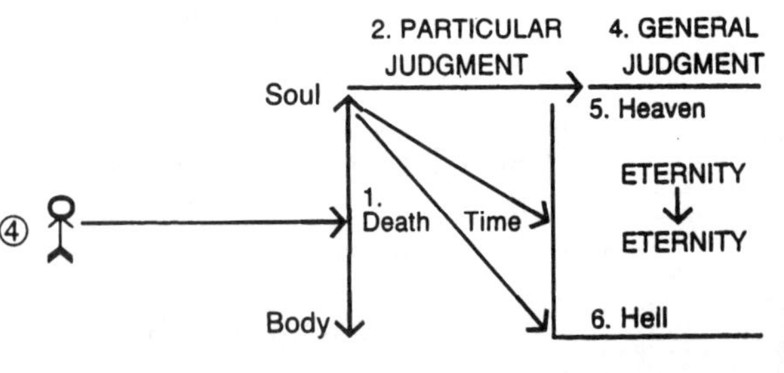
2. PARTICULAR
JUDGMENT
4. GENERAL
JUDGMENT
Soul
5. Heaven
ETERNITY
ETERNITY
④
1.
Death
Time
Body
6. Hell
3. GENERAL
RESURRECTION

* * *

ETERNITY

Life is short, and death is sure.
The hour of death remains obscure.
A soul you have—and only one!
If that be lost, all hope is gone.

Waste not your time, while time shall last.
For after death 'tis ever past.
The all-seeing God your judge will be,
Or Heaven or Hell your destiny.

All earthly things will fleet away,
ETERNITY shall ever stay!

Books
By Rev. Albert J. M. Shamon

Our Lady Teaches About Prayer
at Medjugorje

Our Lady Says: Let Holy Mass Be Your Life

Our Lady Says: Monthly Confession—
Remedy for the West

Our Lady Teaches About Sacramentals
and Blessed Objects

Our Lady Says: Pray the Creed

Three Steps to Sanctity

The Power of the Rosary

Preparing for the Third Millennium

Our Lady Says: Love People

The Ten Commandments of God

Behind the Mass

Apocalypse—The Book For Our Times

Firepower Through Confirmation

Genesis: The Book of Origins

A Graphic Life of Jesus the Christ

The Bishop Sheen We Knew

Reflections on the Encyclical Veritatis Splendor

For additional information, contact CMJ MARIAN
PUBLISHERS, Publishers of Catholic books.

CMJ MARIAN PUBLISHERS
P.O. Box 661, Oak Lawn, Illinois 60454